50 Nut Butter Cookbook Recipes

By: Kelly Johnson

Table of Contents

- Classic Peanut Butter Cookies
- Almond Butter Banana Smoothie
- Cashew Butter Chicken Stir-Fry
- Peanut Butter and Jelly Energy Balls
- Almond Butter Granola Bars
- Hazelnut Butter Chocolate Truffles
- Creamy Peanut Butter Oatmeal
- Cashew Butter Banana Bread
- Peanut Butter and Coconut Energy Bites
- Almond Butter Pancakes
- Chocolate Peanut Butter Smoothie
- Nut Butter Granola
- Cashew Butter and Avocado Toast
- Hazelnut Butter Spread
- Peanut Butter and Chia Seed Pudding
- Almond Butter Stuffed Dates
- Peanut Butter and Jelly Cups
- Cashew Butter Pumpkin Soup
- Almond Butter Carrot Cake Muffins
- Peanut Butter Chocolate Chip Granola
- Nut Butter Protein Balls
- Almond Butter Energy Bars
- Peanut Butter and Banana Toast
- Cashew Butter Zucchini Noodles
- Chocolate Almond Butter Cups
- Peanut Butter Rice Krispies Treats
- Hazelnut Butter Smoothie
- Nut Butter Brownies
- Cashew Butter Chickpea Salad
- Almond Butter Smoothie Bowl
- Peanut Butter and Apple Slices
- Cashew Butter Stuffed Sweet Potatoes
- Nut Butter Banana Split
- Hazelnut Butter French Toast
- Peanut Butter Oatmeal Cookies

- Almond Butter Roasted Vegetables
- Cashew Butter Dip for Veggies
- Peanut Butter Yogurt Parfait
- Hazelnut Butter Hot Chocolate
- Almond Butter Date Bars
- Nut Butter and Fruit Breakfast Wrap
- Peanut Butter Cupcakes
- Cashew Butter Dip with Pretzels
- Almond Butter Popcorn
- Nut Butter Pudding Cups
- Peanut Butter and Chocolate Smoothie
- Cashew Butter Avocado Smoothie
- Almond Butter Muffins
- Hazelnut Butter Chocolate Cake
- Peanut Butter and Banana Smoothie Bowl

Classic Peanut Butter Cookies

Ingredients:

- 1 cup peanut butter
- 1 cup sugar
- 1 egg
- 1 teaspoon vanilla extract
- 1/2 teaspoon baking soda
- A pinch of salt

Instructions:

1. Preheat your oven to 350°F (175°C).
2. In a mixing bowl, combine peanut butter, sugar, egg, vanilla extract, baking soda, and salt. Stir until smooth.
3. Scoop tablespoon-sized portions of dough and roll into balls. Place on a baking sheet lined with parchment paper.
4. Flatten each cookie slightly with a fork, creating a crisscross pattern.
5. Bake for 10-12 minutes, or until the edges are golden brown.
6. Let the cookies cool on a wire rack before serving.

Almond Butter Banana Smoothie

Ingredients:

- 1 ripe banana
- 2 tablespoons almond butter
- 1 cup almond milk (or any milk of choice)
- 1 tablespoon honey (optional)
- 1/2 teaspoon cinnamon
- A pinch of salt

Instructions:

1. Combine all ingredients in a blender.
2. Blend until smooth and creamy.
3. Pour into a glass and enjoy immediately as a healthy and filling smoothie.

Cashew Butter Chicken Stir-Fry

Ingredients:

- 1 lb chicken breast, sliced into strips
- 2 tablespoons cashew butter
- 1 tablespoon soy sauce
- 1 tablespoon sesame oil
- 1/2 teaspoon ginger, grated
- 2 garlic cloves, minced
- 1 bell pepper, sliced
- 1 carrot, julienned
- 1/2 cup cashews, toasted
- Cooked rice, for serving

Instructions:

1. In a bowl, whisk together cashew butter, soy sauce, sesame oil, ginger, and garlic.
2. Heat a skillet over medium-high heat. Add chicken strips and cook until browned and cooked through, about 6-7 minutes. Remove and set aside.
3. In the same skillet, add bell pepper and carrot, cooking for 3-4 minutes until tender.
4. Add the chicken back to the skillet along with the cashew butter sauce. Stir to combine and heat through.
5. Stir in toasted cashews and serve over cooked rice.

Peanut Butter and Jelly Energy Balls

Ingredients:

- 1/2 cup peanut butter
- 1/4 cup honey
- 1 cup rolled oats
- 1/4 cup ground flaxseed
- 1/4 cup jelly or jam (your choice)
- 1/2 teaspoon vanilla extract

Instructions:

1. In a large mixing bowl, combine peanut butter, honey, oats, ground flaxseed, and vanilla extract.
2. Mix until everything is fully combined. Add in the jelly and gently fold it in, creating a marbled effect.
3. Roll the mixture into 1-inch balls and place on a baking sheet lined with parchment paper.
4. Refrigerate for at least 30 minutes before enjoying. Store in an airtight container in the fridge.

Almond Butter Granola Bars

Ingredients:

- 1 cup rolled oats
- 1/2 cup almond butter
- 1/4 cup honey
- 1/2 cup dried fruit (raisins, cranberries, etc.)
- 1/4 cup chopped nuts (almonds, walnuts, etc.)
- 1/2 teaspoon vanilla extract
- A pinch of salt

Instructions:

1. Preheat your oven to 350°F (175°C) and line an 8x8-inch baking pan with parchment paper.
2. In a large bowl, combine oats, dried fruit, chopped nuts, and a pinch of salt.
3. In a small saucepan, heat almond butter and honey over low heat until smooth. Stir in vanilla extract.
4. Pour the almond butter mixture over the dry ingredients and stir to combine.
5. Press the mixture into the prepared baking pan. Bake for 15-20 minutes or until golden brown.
6. Let the bars cool completely before slicing into squares. Store in an airtight container.

Hazelnut Butter Chocolate Truffles

Ingredients:

- 1/2 cup hazelnut butter
- 1/2 cup dark chocolate chips
- 2 tablespoons maple syrup
- 1 teaspoon vanilla extract
- Cocoa powder, for rolling

Instructions:

1. In a heatproof bowl, melt the chocolate chips over a double boiler or in the microwave.
2. Once melted, stir in hazelnut butter, maple syrup, and vanilla extract until smooth.
3. Let the mixture cool slightly, then refrigerate for 30 minutes to firm up.
4. Once chilled, scoop the mixture into small balls and roll them in cocoa powder.
5. Store in an airtight container in the fridge until ready to enjoy.

Creamy Peanut Butter Oatmeal

Ingredients:

- 1/2 cup rolled oats
- 1 cup water or milk (dairy or non-dairy)
- 2 tablespoons peanut butter
- 1 tablespoon honey or maple syrup
- A pinch of salt
- Toppings of your choice (banana slices, granola, etc.)

Instructions:

1. In a saucepan, bring water or milk to a boil. Stir in oats and reduce heat to a simmer.
2. Cook the oats for about 5-7 minutes, stirring occasionally, until the oats are soft and have absorbed most of the liquid.
3. Stir in peanut butter, honey, and salt until creamy and well-mixed.
4. Serve the oatmeal topped with banana slices, granola, or other toppings of your choice.

Cashew Butter Banana Bread

Ingredients:

- 2 ripe bananas, mashed
- 1/2 cup cashew butter
- 1/4 cup honey or maple syrup
- 1 1/2 cups whole wheat flour
- 1 teaspoon baking soda
- 1/2 teaspoon cinnamon
- 1/4 teaspoon salt
- 2 eggs

Instructions:

1. Preheat your oven to 350°F (175°C). Grease a loaf pan or line it with parchment paper.
2. In a bowl, mix mashed bananas, cashew butter, honey, and eggs.
3. In a separate bowl, combine flour, baking soda, cinnamon, and salt.
4. Add the dry ingredients to the wet ingredients and stir until combined.
5. Pour the batter into the prepared loaf pan and bake for 50-60 minutes, or until a toothpick comes out clean.
6. Let the banana bread cool before slicing and serving.

Peanut Butter and Coconut Energy Bites

Ingredients:

- 1/2 cup peanut butter
- 1/4 cup shredded coconut
- 1/2 cup rolled oats
- 1/4 cup honey
- 1/4 teaspoon vanilla extract

Instructions:

1. In a large mixing bowl, combine peanut butter, shredded coconut, oats, honey, and vanilla extract.
2. Stir until well combined and the mixture is sticky.
3. Roll the mixture into 1-inch balls and place them on a parchment-lined baking sheet.
4. Refrigerate for at least 30 minutes before serving. Store in an airtight container.

Almond Butter Pancakes

Ingredients:

- 1 cup almond flour
- 2 eggs
- 1/4 cup almond butter
- 1/4 cup almond milk (or any milk of choice)
- 1 teaspoon vanilla extract
- 1 teaspoon baking powder
- A pinch of salt

Instructions:

1. In a large bowl, whisk together almond flour, eggs, almond butter, almond milk, vanilla extract, baking powder, and salt.
2. Heat a skillet or griddle over medium heat and lightly grease with cooking spray or oil.
3. Pour the batter onto the skillet, forming small pancakes. Cook for 2-3 minutes on each side until golden brown.
4. Serve the pancakes with maple syrup or your favorite toppings.

Chocolate Peanut Butter Smoothie

Ingredients:

- 1 frozen banana
- 2 tablespoons peanut butter
- 1 tablespoon cocoa powder
- 1 cup almond milk (or any milk of choice)
- 1 tablespoon honey or maple syrup (optional)
- A pinch of salt
- Ice cubes (optional)

Instructions:

1. Combine all ingredients in a blender.
2. Blend until smooth and creamy.
3. Pour into a glass and serve immediately as a refreshing and indulgent smoothie.

Nut Butter Granola

Ingredients:

- 2 cups rolled oats
- 1/2 cup almond butter (or any nut butter)
- 1/4 cup honey or maple syrup
- 1/4 cup coconut oil, melted
- 1/4 cup chopped nuts (such as almonds, walnuts, or pecans)
- 1/2 teaspoon cinnamon
- A pinch of salt
- 1/4 cup dried fruit (optional)

Instructions:

1. Preheat your oven to 350°F (175°C) and line a baking sheet with parchment paper.
2. In a large bowl, combine oats, nuts, cinnamon, and salt.
3. In a separate bowl, mix together almond butter, honey, and melted coconut oil.
4. Pour the wet ingredients over the dry ingredients and stir until everything is evenly coated.
5. Spread the granola mixture on the baking sheet in an even layer.
6. Bake for 20-25 minutes, stirring halfway through, until golden and crispy.
7. Let the granola cool completely before stirring in dried fruit, if using. Store in an airtight container.

Cashew Butter and Avocado Toast

Ingredients:

- 2 slices of whole-grain bread
- 2 tablespoons cashew butter
- 1 ripe avocado, mashed
- Salt and pepper, to taste
- Red pepper flakes (optional)
- Lemon juice (optional)

Instructions:

1. Toast the bread slices to your desired level of crispiness.
2. Spread 1 tablespoon of cashew butter on each slice of toasted bread.
3. Top with mashed avocado, and sprinkle with salt, pepper, and red pepper flakes.
4. Drizzle with lemon juice for extra flavor, if desired. Serve immediately.

Hazelnut Butter Spread

Ingredients:

- 1 cup roasted hazelnuts
- 2 tablespoons honey or maple syrup
- 1/2 teaspoon vanilla extract
- A pinch of salt

Instructions:

1. In a food processor, pulse the roasted hazelnuts until a smooth butter forms, scraping down the sides as needed.
2. Add honey or maple syrup, vanilla extract, and salt, and continue processing until smooth and creamy.
3. Transfer the spread to a jar and store in the refrigerator for up to 2 weeks.

Peanut Butter and Chia Seed Pudding

Ingredients:

- 2 tablespoons peanut butter
- 1 tablespoon chia seeds
- 1 cup almond milk (or any milk of choice)
- 1 tablespoon honey or maple syrup (optional)
- 1/2 teaspoon vanilla extract

Instructions:

1. In a jar or bowl, whisk together peanut butter, almond milk, honey, and vanilla extract.
2. Stir in chia seeds and mix well.
3. Cover and refrigerate for at least 4 hours or overnight, allowing the chia seeds to absorb the liquid and form a pudding-like texture.
4. Serve topped with fresh fruit or nuts if desired.

Almond Butter Stuffed Dates

Ingredients:

- 10 Medjool dates, pitted
- 1/4 cup almond butter
- A pinch of sea salt (optional)
- Chopped dark chocolate or cocoa nibs (optional)

Instructions:

1. Slice each date in half and remove the pit.
2. Fill each date with a teaspoon of almond butter.
3. Sprinkle with sea salt, if desired, and top with chopped dark chocolate or cocoa nibs.
4. Serve as a snack or dessert. Store in an airtight container.

Peanut Butter and Jelly Cups

Ingredients:

- 1/2 cup peanut butter
- 1/4 cup jelly or jam of your choice
- 1/2 cup dark chocolate chips
- 1 tablespoon coconut oil

Instructions:

1. Line a mini muffin tin with paper liners.
2. In a microwave-safe bowl, melt the chocolate chips with coconut oil in 20-second intervals, stirring between, until smooth.
3. Spoon a small amount of melted chocolate into each muffin cup, just enough to cover the bottom.
4. Freeze for 10 minutes to set the chocolate.
5. After the chocolate has hardened, add a spoonful of peanut butter and a small spoonful of jelly on top.
6. Finish by covering the peanut butter and jelly layer with more melted chocolate.
7. Freeze again for about 30 minutes or until set. Enjoy!

Cashew Butter Pumpkin Soup

Ingredients:

- 1 tablespoon olive oil
- 1 small onion, chopped
- 2 cups pumpkin puree
- 2 cups vegetable broth
- 1/2 cup cashew butter
- 1 teaspoon ground cinnamon
- 1/2 teaspoon ground ginger
- Salt and pepper, to taste

Instructions:

1. Heat olive oil in a large pot over medium heat. Add chopped onion and sauté until soft, about 5 minutes.
2. Stir in pumpkin puree, vegetable broth, cashew butter, cinnamon, ginger, salt, and pepper.
3. Bring the mixture to a simmer and cook for 10 minutes, stirring occasionally.
4. Use an immersion blender or transfer to a blender to puree the soup until smooth.
5. Serve hot with a drizzle of extra cashew butter, if desired.

Almond Butter Carrot Cake Muffins

Ingredients:

- 1 1/2 cups almond flour
- 1 teaspoon baking soda
- 1/2 teaspoon cinnamon
- 1/4 teaspoon nutmeg
- 1/4 teaspoon salt
- 2 eggs
- 1/4 cup almond butter
- 1/4 cup honey or maple syrup
- 1 teaspoon vanilla extract
- 1 cup grated carrots
- 1/4 cup raisins (optional)
- 1/4 cup chopped walnuts (optional)

Instructions:

1. Preheat your oven to 350°F (175°C) and line a muffin tin with paper liners.
2. In a large bowl, combine almond flour, baking soda, cinnamon, nutmeg, and salt.
3. In a separate bowl, whisk together eggs, almond butter, honey, and vanilla extract.
4. Add the wet ingredients to the dry ingredients and mix until well combined.
5. Stir in grated carrots, raisins, and walnuts (if using).
6. Divide the batter evenly into the muffin cups and bake for 18-20 minutes, or until a toothpick inserted into the center comes out clean.
7. Let the muffins cool before serving.

Peanut Butter Chocolate Chip Granola

Ingredients:

- 2 cups rolled oats
- 1/2 cup peanut butter
- 1/4 cup honey or maple syrup
- 1/4 cup coconut oil, melted
- 1/2 cup dark chocolate chips
- 1/4 cup chopped nuts (optional)
- 1/2 teaspoon vanilla extract
- A pinch of salt

Instructions:

1. Preheat your oven to 350°F (175°C) and line a baking sheet with parchment paper.
2. In a large bowl, combine oats, melted coconut oil, honey, peanut butter, vanilla extract, and salt. Mix until everything is evenly coated.
3. Spread the mixture on the baking sheet in an even layer.
4. Bake for 20-25 minutes, stirring halfway through, until golden and crispy.
5. Once cooled, stir in chocolate chips and chopped nuts, if using.
6. Store in an airtight container.

Nut Butter Protein Balls

Ingredients:

- 1 cup almond butter (or any nut butter)
- 1/2 cup rolled oats
- 1/4 cup protein powder
- 1/4 cup honey or maple syrup
- 1/4 cup mini chocolate chips (optional)
- 1 teaspoon vanilla extract
- A pinch of salt

Instructions:

1. In a large bowl, combine all ingredients.
2. Stir until fully mixed and a dough-like consistency forms.
3. Roll into 1-inch balls and place them on a parchment-lined baking sheet.
4. Refrigerate for at least 30 minutes to firm up.
5. Store in the fridge for up to a week.

Almond Butter Energy Bars

Ingredients:

- 1 cup almond butter
- 1/2 cup rolled oats
- 1/2 cup dried fruit (raisins, cranberries, or apricots)
- 1/4 cup honey or maple syrup
- 1/4 cup chia seeds or flaxseeds
- 1/4 cup mini chocolate chips (optional)
- 1 teaspoon vanilla extract

Instructions:

1. In a bowl, mix almond butter, honey, and vanilla extract.
2. Add oats, dried fruit, chia seeds, and chocolate chips, and stir to combine.
3. Press the mixture into a greased or parchment-lined baking pan.
4. Refrigerate for at least 2 hours to set.
5. Cut into bars and store in the fridge for up to a week.

Peanut Butter and Banana Toast

Ingredients:

- 2 slices of whole-grain bread, toasted
- 2 tablespoons peanut butter
- 1 banana, sliced
- A sprinkle of cinnamon (optional)
- A drizzle of honey (optional)

Instructions:

1. Toast the bread slices to your desired crispiness.
2. Spread peanut butter evenly on each slice of toast.
3. Top with banana slices.
4. Sprinkle with cinnamon and drizzle with honey for added flavor.
5. Serve immediately.

Cashew Butter Zucchini Noodles

Ingredients:

- 2 medium zucchinis, spiralized into noodles
- 1/4 cup cashew butter
- 2 tablespoons olive oil
- 1 tablespoon lemon juice
- 1 tablespoon nutritional yeast (optional)
- Salt and pepper to taste
- Fresh parsley, chopped (optional)

Instructions:

1. In a small bowl, whisk together cashew butter, olive oil, lemon juice, nutritional yeast, salt, and pepper.
2. Toss the zucchini noodles with the cashew butter sauce until evenly coated.
3. Garnish with fresh parsley, if desired, and serve immediately.

Chocolate Almond Butter Cups

Ingredients:

- 1/2 cup almond butter
- 1/4 cup dark chocolate chips
- 2 tablespoons coconut oil
- 1 tablespoon maple syrup or honey
- A pinch of sea salt

Instructions:

1. Line a muffin tin with paper liners.
2. In a microwave-safe bowl, melt chocolate chips with coconut oil in 20-second intervals, stirring between, until smooth.
3. Spoon a small amount of melted chocolate into each muffin cup, just enough to cover the bottom.
4. Place the tin in the freezer for about 10 minutes to harden.
5. Once set, spoon almond butter on top of the hardened chocolate layer.
6. Top with the remaining melted chocolate and sprinkle with a pinch of sea salt.
7. Freeze again for 20-30 minutes to set completely.
8. Enjoy as a sweet treat!

Peanut Butter Rice Krispies Treats

Ingredients:

- 3 cups Rice Krispies cereal
- 1/2 cup peanut butter
- 1/4 cup honey or maple syrup
- 1 teaspoon vanilla extract
- A pinch of salt

Instructions:

1. In a large pot, melt peanut butter, honey, and vanilla extract over low heat, stirring until smooth.
2. Remove from heat and stir in Rice Krispies cereal until fully coated.
3. Press the mixture into a greased or parchment-lined baking dish.
4. Let it cool at room temperature before cutting into squares.
5. Store in an airtight container.

Hazelnut Butter Smoothie

Ingredients:

- 1 frozen banana
- 1 tablespoon hazelnut butter
- 1/2 cup almond milk (or any milk of choice)
- 1 tablespoon honey or maple syrup (optional)
- 1/2 teaspoon vanilla extract
- Ice cubes (optional)

Instructions:

1. Combine all ingredients in a blender.
2. Blend until smooth and creamy.
3. Pour into a glass and serve immediately as a refreshing smoothie.

Nut Butter Brownies

Ingredients:

- 1/2 cup almond butter (or any nut butter)
- 1/2 cup cocoa powder
- 1/2 cup honey or maple syrup
- 2 eggs
- 1 teaspoon vanilla extract
- 1/4 cup dark chocolate chips (optional)
- A pinch of salt

Instructions:

1. Preheat your oven to 350°F (175°C) and grease a baking pan.
2. In a bowl, mix together almond butter, cocoa powder, honey, eggs, vanilla extract, and salt.
3. Fold in chocolate chips, if using.
4. Pour the batter into the prepared pan and smooth the top.
5. Bake for 20-25 minutes, or until a toothpick inserted into the center comes out clean.
6. Let the brownies cool before slicing and serving.

Cashew Butter Chickpea Salad

Ingredients:

- 1 can (15 oz) chickpeas, drained and rinsed
- 2 tablespoons cashew butter
- 1 tablespoon olive oil
- 1 tablespoon lemon juice
- 1/4 teaspoon garlic powder
- Salt and pepper, to taste
- 1/4 cup red onion, finely diced
- 1/4 cup cucumber, diced
- 1/4 cup cherry tomatoes, halved
- Fresh parsley, chopped (optional)

Instructions:

1. In a bowl, combine chickpeas, red onion, cucumber, and tomatoes.
2. In a separate small bowl, whisk together cashew butter, olive oil, lemon juice, garlic powder, salt, and pepper until smooth.
3. Pour the dressing over the salad and toss gently to combine.
4. Garnish with fresh parsley, if desired.
5. Serve chilled or at room temperature.

Almond Butter Smoothie Bowl

Ingredients:

- 1 frozen banana
- 1/2 cup almond butter
- 1/2 cup almond milk (or any milk of choice)
- 1/4 cup Greek yogurt (optional for added creaminess)
- 1 tablespoon honey or maple syrup (optional)
- Toppings: granola, fresh fruit, coconut flakes, chia seeds, nuts, etc.

Instructions:

1. Blend frozen banana, almond butter, almond milk, Greek yogurt, and honey in a blender until smooth.
2. Pour into a bowl and top with your favorite toppings such as granola, fresh fruit, coconut flakes, or nuts.
3. Serve immediately for a delicious breakfast or snack.

Peanut Butter and Apple Slices

Ingredients:

- 1 apple, sliced
- 2 tablespoons peanut butter
- A sprinkle of cinnamon (optional)
- Chopped nuts (optional)

Instructions:

1. Slice the apple into rounds or wedges.
2. Spread a thin layer of peanut butter on each apple slice.
3. Sprinkle with cinnamon and chopped nuts, if desired.
4. Serve immediately as a quick, healthy snack.

Cashew Butter Stuffed Sweet Potatoes

Ingredients:

- 2 medium sweet potatoes
- 2 tablespoons cashew butter
- 1 tablespoon maple syrup or honey
- A pinch of cinnamon
- A pinch of salt
- Chopped pecans or walnuts (optional)

Instructions:

1. Preheat your oven to 400°F (200°C). Pierce sweet potatoes with a fork and bake for 40-45 minutes, or until tender.
2. Slice the cooked sweet potatoes open and fluff the insides with a fork.
3. Drizzle with cashew butter, maple syrup, cinnamon, and a pinch of salt.
4. Top with chopped nuts, if desired.
5. Serve immediately as a delicious and filling meal.

Nut Butter Banana Split

Ingredients:

- 1 banana, sliced lengthwise
- 2 tablespoons peanut butter (or any nut butter)
- 1/2 cup Greek yogurt or whipped cream
- Fresh berries (strawberries, blueberries, raspberries)
- Dark chocolate chips (optional)
- Chopped nuts (optional)

Instructions:

1. Slice the banana lengthwise and arrange on a plate.
2. Drizzle peanut butter over the banana.
3. Top with Greek yogurt or whipped cream.
4. Add fresh berries, chocolate chips, and chopped nuts as toppings.
5. Serve immediately as a healthy take on the classic banana split.

Hazelnut Butter French Toast

Ingredients:

- 2 slices of bread (preferably thick-cut)
- 2 eggs
- 1/4 cup milk (or any milk of choice)
- 1 tablespoon hazelnut butter
- 1 teaspoon cinnamon
- 1/2 teaspoon vanilla extract
- Maple syrup, for serving
- Fresh berries (optional)

Instructions:

1. In a bowl, whisk together eggs, milk, cinnamon, and vanilla extract.
2. Heat a non-stick skillet over medium heat and lightly grease with cooking spray or butter.
3. Spread hazelnut butter on one side of each slice of bread.
4. Dip the bread slices into the egg mixture, coating both sides, and cook in the skillet until golden brown on both sides, about 3-4 minutes per side.
5. Serve with maple syrup and fresh berries.

Peanut Butter Oatmeal Cookies

Ingredients:

- 1/2 cup peanut butter
- 1/2 cup rolled oats
- 1/4 cup honey or maple syrup
- 1/2 cup whole wheat flour
- 1 egg
- 1 teaspoon vanilla extract
- A pinch of salt
- 1/4 cup dark chocolate chips (optional)

Instructions:

1. Preheat your oven to 350°F (175°C) and line a baking sheet with parchment paper.
2. In a bowl, combine peanut butter, oats, honey, flour, egg, vanilla extract, and salt. Mix until well combined.
3. Fold in chocolate chips, if using.
4. Scoop tablespoon-sized portions of dough and roll into balls. Place them on the baking sheet and flatten slightly with a fork.
5. Bake for 8-10 minutes, or until golden brown.
6. Let them cool on the baking sheet for 5 minutes before transferring to a wire rack to cool completely.

Almond Butter Roasted Vegetables

Ingredients:

- 2 cups mixed vegetables (carrots, broccoli, cauliflower, bell peppers, etc.)
- 2 tablespoons almond butter
- 1 tablespoon olive oil
- 1 tablespoon soy sauce or tamari
- 1 tablespoon honey or maple syrup
- 1 teaspoon garlic powder
- A pinch of salt and pepper

Instructions:

1. Preheat your oven to 400°F (200°C).
2. In a small bowl, whisk together almond butter, olive oil, soy sauce, honey, garlic powder, salt, and pepper until smooth.
3. Toss the vegetables with the almond butter mixture until evenly coated.
4. Spread the vegetables in a single layer on a baking sheet.
5. Roast for 20-25 minutes, flipping halfway through, until tender and lightly browned.
6. Serve immediately as a side dish or light main course.

Cashew Butter Dip for Veggies

Ingredients:

- 1/2 cup cashew butter
- 1/4 cup Greek yogurt or coconut yogurt
- 1 tablespoon lemon juice
- 1 tablespoon olive oil
- 1 clove garlic, minced
- Salt and pepper, to taste
- Fresh herbs (like parsley or dill), optional

Instructions:

1. In a bowl, combine cashew butter, Greek yogurt, lemon juice, olive oil, and garlic.
2. Stir until smooth, adding salt and pepper to taste.
3. Serve with fresh veggies like carrots, cucumber, and bell peppers for dipping.

Peanut Butter Yogurt Parfait

Ingredients:

- 1/2 cup peanut butter
- 1 cup Greek yogurt
- 2 tablespoons honey or maple syrup
- 1/4 cup granola
- Fresh fruit (like bananas or berries)

Instructions:

1. In a bowl, mix together peanut butter, Greek yogurt, and honey until smooth.
2. Layer the yogurt mixture in a glass or bowl with granola and fresh fruit.
3. Repeat layers, finishing with a topping of granola and fruit.
4. Serve immediately or refrigerate for a few hours for a cool snack.

Hazelnut Butter Hot Chocolate

Ingredients:

- 2 tablespoons hazelnut butter
- 1 1/2 cups milk (or any dairy-free milk)
- 2 tablespoons cocoa powder
- 2 tablespoons maple syrup or sugar (to taste)
- 1/2 teaspoon vanilla extract
- A pinch of salt

Instructions:

1. In a small saucepan, heat the milk over medium heat.
2. Stir in the hazelnut butter, cocoa powder, maple syrup, vanilla extract, and salt until fully combined and smooth.
3. Heat until hot, but do not bring to a boil.
4. Pour into a mug and serve warm, garnished with whipped cream or marshmallows if desired.

Almond Butter Date Bars

Ingredients:

- 1 cup almond butter
- 1 cup rolled oats
- 1/2 cup pitted dates, chopped
- 2 tablespoons honey or maple syrup
- 1/4 teaspoon vanilla extract
- 1/4 teaspoon cinnamon (optional)
- A pinch of salt

Instructions:

1. In a food processor, pulse the oats, dates, almond butter, honey, vanilla extract, cinnamon, and salt until the mixture is well combined and sticky.
2. Press the mixture into a lined baking pan, smoothing it out evenly.
3. Refrigerate for at least 2 hours or until firm.
4. Slice into bars and serve. Store in the refrigerator for up to a week.

Nut Butter and Fruit Breakfast Wrap

Ingredients:

- 1 whole wheat tortilla or wrap
- 2 tablespoons almond butter (or any nut butter)
- 1/2 banana, sliced
- 1/4 cup fresh berries (like strawberries or blueberries)
- A drizzle of honey (optional)

Instructions:

1. Spread the almond butter evenly over the tortilla.
2. Layer with sliced banana and fresh berries.
3. Drizzle with honey, if desired.
4. Roll up the tortilla and slice into wraps. Serve immediately for a quick breakfast or snack.

Peanut Butter Cupcakes

Ingredients:

- 1 cup flour
- 1/2 cup peanut butter
- 1/2 cup sugar (or sweetener of choice)
- 1/2 teaspoon baking soda
- 1/4 teaspoon salt
- 1 egg
- 1/4 cup milk (or any milk of choice)
- 1/4 cup melted butter or oil
- 1 teaspoon vanilla extract

Instructions:

1. Preheat your oven to 350°F (175°C) and line a muffin tin with cupcake liners.
2. In a bowl, whisk together flour, sugar, baking soda, and salt.
3. In another bowl, mix together peanut butter, egg, milk, melted butter, and vanilla extract.
4. Combine the wet and dry ingredients, stirring until smooth.
5. Spoon the batter into the cupcake liners, filling each about 2/3 full.
6. Bake for 18-20 minutes or until a toothpick comes out clean.
7. Allow to cool before serving.

Cashew Butter Dip with Pretzels

Ingredients:

- 1/2 cup cashew butter
- 2 tablespoons honey or maple syrup
- 1/4 teaspoon cinnamon (optional)
- A pinch of salt
- Pretzels (for dipping)

Instructions:

1. In a bowl, whisk together cashew butter, honey, cinnamon, and a pinch of salt until smooth.
2. Serve with pretzels for dipping, and enjoy this sweet and savory snack.

Almond Butter Popcorn

Ingredients:

- 1/4 cup almond butter
- 1 tablespoon coconut oil or butter
- 1 tablespoon maple syrup or honey
- 1/4 teaspoon cinnamon (optional)
- 6 cups popped popcorn (about 1/2 cup unpopped kernels)

Instructions:

1. In a small saucepan, melt the almond butter, coconut oil, and maple syrup together over low heat, stirring until smooth.
2. Drizzle the almond butter mixture over the popcorn and toss to coat evenly.
3. Sprinkle with cinnamon, if desired, and serve immediately.

Nut Butter Pudding Cups

Ingredients:

- 1/2 cup peanut butter (or any nut butter)
- 1/2 cup Greek yogurt
- 2 tablespoons cocoa powder
- 1-2 tablespoons honey or maple syrup (to taste)
- A pinch of salt
- Dark chocolate shavings or crushed nuts for garnish

Instructions:

1. In a bowl, mix peanut butter, Greek yogurt, cocoa powder, honey, and a pinch of salt until smooth.
2. Spoon the pudding mixture into small cups or jars.
3. Refrigerate for 1-2 hours to firm up.
4. Garnish with dark chocolate shavings or crushed nuts before serving.

Peanut Butter and Chocolate Smoothie

Ingredients:

- 1 banana
- 2 tablespoons peanut butter
- 1 tablespoon cocoa powder
- 1 cup milk (or any milk alternative)
- 1/2 teaspoon vanilla extract
- Ice cubes (optional)

Instructions:

1. In a blender, combine the banana, peanut butter, cocoa powder, milk, vanilla extract, and ice cubes (if using).
2. Blend until smooth and creamy.
3. Pour into a glass and enjoy a rich, chocolatey smoothie.

Cashew Butter Avocado Smoothie

Ingredients:

- 1/2 avocado
- 2 tablespoons cashew butter
- 1 cup almond milk (or any milk alternative)
- 1 tablespoon honey or maple syrup
- 1/2 teaspoon vanilla extract
- Ice cubes (optional)

Instructions:

1. In a blender, add the avocado, cashew butter, almond milk, honey, vanilla extract, and ice cubes (if desired).
2. Blend until smooth and creamy.
3. Pour into a glass and serve immediately.

Almond Butter Muffins

Ingredients:

- 1 1/2 cups whole wheat flour
- 1/2 cup almond butter
- 1/2 cup maple syrup or honey
- 1/2 cup milk (or any milk alternative)
- 1 egg
- 1 teaspoon vanilla extract
- 1 teaspoon baking powder
- 1/4 teaspoon baking soda
- 1/4 teaspoon salt
- 1/2 cup chopped nuts or chocolate chips (optional)

Instructions:

1. Preheat your oven to 350°F (175°C) and line a muffin tin with paper liners.
2. In a large bowl, whisk together the flour, baking powder, baking soda, and salt.
3. In another bowl, mix almond butter, maple syrup, milk, egg, and vanilla extract until smooth.
4. Combine the wet and dry ingredients and stir until just combined. If desired, fold in the nuts or chocolate chips.
5. Divide the batter evenly into the muffin tin.
6. Bake for 18-20 minutes or until a toothpick comes out clean.
7. Let cool before serving.

Hazelnut Butter Chocolate Cake

Ingredients:

- 1 cup hazelnut butter
- 1/2 cup cocoa powder
- 1/2 cup maple syrup or honey
- 2 eggs
- 1 teaspoon vanilla extract
- 1/2 cup almond flour (or regular flour)
- 1/4 teaspoon baking soda
- A pinch of salt
- 1/2 cup dark chocolate chips (optional)

Instructions:

1. Preheat your oven to 350°F (175°C) and grease an 8-inch cake pan.
2. In a large bowl, whisk together hazelnut butter, cocoa powder, maple syrup, eggs, and vanilla extract until smooth.
3. Add almond flour, baking soda, and salt, and mix until combined.
4. If using, fold in dark chocolate chips.
5. Pour the batter into the prepared cake pan and smooth the top.
6. Bake for 25-30 minutes or until a toothpick comes out clean.
7. Let the cake cool in the pan for 10 minutes before transferring it to a wire rack to cool completely.

Peanut Butter and Banana Smoothie Bowl

Ingredients:

- 1 banana, frozen
- 2 tablespoons peanut butter
- 1/2 cup almond milk (or any milk alternative)
- 1 tablespoon honey or maple syrup
- Toppings: sliced bananas, granola, chia seeds, nuts, or coconut flakes

Instructions:

1. In a blender, combine the frozen banana, peanut butter, almond milk, and honey.
2. Blend until smooth and thick, adding more milk if needed.
3. Pour the smoothie into a bowl and top with your favorite toppings like sliced bananas, granola, chia seeds, or nuts.
4. Serve immediately for a refreshing breakfast or snack.

www.ingramcontent.com/pod-product-compliance
Lightning Source LLC
LaVergne TN
LVHW081342060526
838201LV00055B/2805